The Witches Manifesto

The Time Is Now

By AMA

Using my magic to honor the important women who raised me

Joyce, Dani, Lynn
Mimi, Mom, Auntie Bea
Auntie Rosemary, Tantina, Janis
Auntie Margaret, Auntie Mamie

AWAKE

I woke to the sound of drums in my ear and the swirl of vomit in my belly.
I had asked for a sign to call myself a Nature Witch. Asked how best to use this gift to honor the important women in my life.

It had Arrived.

Now ~ Right Now ~ 4am ~ was the time to decide. Crawl out into the cold wet meadow, barf, cuddle back in and Sleep or Wake up and Write out what was twisting in my Belly.

Oh how Naive to make a deal with the Universe. She kept me up all night with her wily ways but in the end with the hoot of owl in my other ear
we birthed a book.
And so it begins...Our story of a Nature Witch and her Message to Share.

The Time is NOW

I write this book in the dark of night surrounded by the sounds of nature. I can smell the Magic in the air. Taste it on my lips.

How does it feel?
        How do I feel?

        Excited   Powerful   Bold

All you out there drawn to Witchy Ways ~ you are probably a witch too.
        Who were your
                ancestors?
Who just showed up in your thoughts?

        My grandpa was a warlock.
His mother a midwife.

        It's in your blood somewhere
          Claim It.

The Witches Manifesto

MANIFESTO

Witches at Heart
Humanity
needs us.
Be Brave step out of the
Shadows of Silence & Shyness

Join Us
In Accepting Ourselves
Step into our creative center
Unite Together
Entice the Stuck
Heal with Heart
Nurture Nature

Take Action
The Time is Now

ACCEPT

I am a Nature Witch ~ My Magical Power is creating beautiful personalized outdoor garden spaces where people can Relax, Recharge, Inspire.
A place to Heal
Take a Deep Breath.
What resonates with you?
What do people admire about you?
What are you drawn to?

What is your magical power?

crafty	nourishing	creative	legal	dance
coder	political	smart	innovative	speaking
humor	hugs	healing	scientific	writing
design	innovative	loving	finance	mathematics

... So many more ~ name it ~ claim it

Who am I?
Who I am?
Shazam
Just like that you know the answer
Easy ~ So Easy

STEP IN

Create your Space ~ Take your Time
Sit with Creativity
Boomerang out a small ask
When it comes back ~ know it's real
See it can be done
Stretch out your Comfort Zone
Step out into it
Don't Hesitate
Our beautiful world is waiting
Peace on Earth is a Project ~ not a Promise
Such a fun project to be had
Embrace it in your own way
With your love, your skills, your passion
Ask how can you Create
Ask how can you Heal
Ask how can you Help
Boomerang that out into the Universe.

UNITE

It will take All of our connections ~ All of our Courage to move
Forward into our Future Frontier

Pinchy Pinchy little Witchy. Time to Wake Up.
Wiggle Wiggle Wiggle ~ Wiggle Wiggle Wiggle
The Time is Now
Gather your people ~ Come as you are
Our Planet has been waiting
It's Time for Transformation
Evolution Revolution
Tickle Tickle Tickle ~ Tickle Tickle Tickle
Flip the Switch ~ Try the Top
with Courage not Fear
with Heart not Hate
with Justice not Judgement
with Thoughtfulness not Thriftiness
Trade in your Shyness for Shenanigans
Young and Old
Unite

ENTICE

One good deed deserves another
engage with humanity
keep them spellbound with love
A little Magic goes a long way...

Small Smirk
Bubbly Heart
Good Intention
the breath catches in my throat when it happens
Make me Laugh ~ Make me Smile
Feel your Power
use it Correctly and with Honor
Pass it on
there is

~ Plenty ~

HEAL

This is where it all Begins and where it all Ends.
Helping ourselves allows us to help
each Other.
The more we Heal the Lighter we Feel
the Lighter we Feel the more Grounded we Become.

It is Time to Light the Candle of Love
let it shine in all the

Scary Dark Places

Unshackle the Shame
Release the Hatred
Give up the Greed
Unanchor the Abuse
Befriend thyself ~ Take the Hand
Call the Pyres of the Past to Illuminate our Path
Lead out from temptation and into

Action

Dive In
It's Magical

Dive in to the Depths of our World
There is so much Beauty Waiting
Dive in with your Heart Open and
Singing
Gather those who will be gathered
Come Together
let us create
Beauty
Joy
Laughter

FOR ALL

IF

YOU

DARE

The Hidden Witches Workbook

Wait!!

Easy Spell book

As Simple as can Be
wiggle ~ wiggle ~ wiggle

Just a few quick answers needed to assist you on your internal journey. Find clarity and insight into your sense of purpose for our future frontier.
These questions work best if you note the first thing that comes to mind...

What are 3 activities that you love doing so much you lose track of time when doing them?

_____   _____   _____

What are 3 skills that come easy to you?

_____   _____   _____

Three Values you feel strongly about?

_____   _____   _____

Three Passions or something you have always been interested in learning?

_____

_____

_____

What are a few of the biggest challenges and problems that you see in the world that hurt your heart?

_____

_____

_____

Circle one of these issues you would you like to put your magic towards?

Name one small step you could take this week to help.

The Good Life Includes ~ people places things ~ list 5 or 6.

_____   _____   _____

_____   _____   _____

Shhhhh ~ Secret Idea you have…..

Name one small step you can take this week to get started on your Secret Idea

Lets make some room .....

What negative emotion would you like to
      Unshackle ~Give Up ~ Release???

          _____

              Who do
               You
            want to forgive?

       _____

       What action will you do that will help you
            release negativity and remind you
                of your path forward

_____light candle   _____deep breath   ____journal

____meditate   _____gratitude thought   _____laugh

_____affirmation   other _____   _____ all

Living the Dream ~ What does that look like? Ted Talk? Oprah? You're Playing with Magic!
Three Asks of the Good Life you want to Boomerang out to the Universe. Be Specific Ask for exactly what you Desire...

_____

_____

_____

6 words to describe the Highest Vision of your most Magical and Powerful Self.

_____   _____   _____

_____   _____   _____

Circle 1 or 2 sentences in this book that are sticking with you. Take a walk with them and see where they lead.

A handful of helpful prompts to ponder if you are stuck

1. What brings me joy and fulfillment? Consider the activities and experiences that bring you the most joy and fulfillment. This could include spending time in nature, practicing certain healing modalities, or engaging in creative pursuits.

2. What are my unique strengths and talents? Reflect on your natural strengths and talents, Consider how you can use these strengths to make a positive impact in the world.

3. What challenges have I overcome in my life, and how can I use them to help others? Think about the challenges and struggles you have faced in your life, and how they have shaped you into the person you are today. Consider how you can use these experiences to support and uplift others who may be going through similar challenges.

4. What values are most important to me? Reflect on the values that guide your life, such as compassion, integrity, honesty, or social justice. Consider how you can use these values to make a positive impact in the world.

5. What can I be paid for? Consider how you can sustain yourself financially while pursuing your healing work. This could include offering paid services, creating products, or finding other ways to monetize your skills and passions.

6. What do I want my legacy to be? Consider the impact you want to have on the world and the legacy you want to leave behind. This could include inspiring others to follow their own paths, creating positive change in your community, or making a difference on a global scale.

By exploring these different questions, a good witch can gain a deeper understanding of her Ikigai and find a sense of purpose and fulfillment in her practice.

If you have Searched Deeply for the Answers
in this Witchy Workbook
you are now well on your way in joining our
Caring Coven of Community.
So many people want to Heal this Planet
but just don't know where to start.
Pass this Magical Manifesto on to Many.
It will land exactly where and how it should.

About the Author

Anne-Marie Allen has been a land designer for over 30 years. She has recently founded the non~profit
Deep Breath Healing Gardens which installs small personalized healing spaces for people undergoing Cancer Treatment.
Proceeds from the sale of this
Manifesto
will help fund these
wonderful gardens spaces

You can also check out her webpages.
www.deepbreathgardens.com
www.allenlanddesign.com

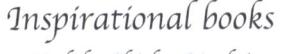

Inspirational books
Out on a Limb by Shirley Maclaine
https://www.goodreads.com/book/show/110349.Out_on_a_Limb

Big magic by Elizabeth Gilbert
https://www.elizabethgilbert.com/books/big-magic/

Five Second Rule by Mel Robbins
https://www.melrobbins.com/5secondrule

Chill and Prosper by Denise Duffield-Thomas
https://www.denisedt.com/prosper

The Witches Manifesto is a call to action. Peace on Earth is a Project not a Promise Such a fun Project to be had ~ embraced in your own way.

Written in the middle of the night assisted by pure inspiration ~ a Gift from the Universe~ this book first awakens & acknowledges the urge for good, helpful action towards Humanity and our Planet then easily guides the reader on a journey to find their passion, use their skills and take steps to help us get this Evolution Revolution started!

It's about time. You, the reader, know this.

Dive In ~ It's Magical

www.ingramcontent.com/pod-product-compliance
Lightning Source LLC
Chambersburg PA
CBHW041506010526
44118CB00001B/30